Samuel Finley Breese Morse

The Present Attempt to Dissolve the American Union

A British Aristocratic Plot

Samuel Finley Breese Morse

The Present Attempt to Dissolve the American Union
A British Aristocratic Plot

ISBN/EAN: 9783337008314

Printed in Europe, USA, Canada, Australia, Japan

Cover: Foto ©Suzi / pixelio.de

More available books at **www.hansebooks.com**

THE

PRESENT ATTEMPT

TO

DISSOLVE THE AMERICAN UNION,

A British Aristocratic Plot.

BY

B.

NEW YORK:

PRINTED FOR THE AUTHOR.

JOHN F. TROW, 50 GREENE STREET.

1862.

PREFATORY REMARKS.

THE first of this series of papers, it will be observed, and that which prompted all the rest, was published in *Harper's Weekly* in Dec. 1860. It was not an anonymous paper, but its statements were vouched for by a responsible name, Sidney E. Morse, Esq., the originator of the Religious Newspaper, and for many years the distinguished and indefatigable editor of the New York *Observer*. The flippant and personally disparaging notice, in the New York *Tribune*, of Mr. Morse's narrative of the important facts which came under his own cognizance, aroused the indignation of many persons, the writer of these papers among the rest, and having coincident facts from his own observation and research, he deemed it to be his duty as a patriot, to bring them forward at this time, not merely for the purpose of defending Mr. Morse from the ungenerous attacks made upon him by the *Tribune*, but for the more important purpose of drawing public attention to what he believes to be the main political cause of our national troubles. The writer does not mean to say that to British Intrigues are due all the excitement and ill blood which are now so sadly dominant in the country, for there was a predisposition, doubtless, in many influential American minds, favorably adapted to the action of these intrigues, furnishing indeed the basis of, and inviting, this action; but he does intend to say that British politicians have adroitly taken advantage of this state of feeling, and by artfully and assiduously increasing the excitement, have used it to accomplish their great measure of State policy, *the severance of the United States.*

In all that relates to *African Slavery,* Great Britain has ever taken a most prominent part, long before the era of our national independence. Every measure of that Government, whether in favor of slavery or against slavery, has been enacted by her, directly or indirectly, for the promotion of her own material interests, and chiefly to increase or maintain the power of her oligarchy. At different periods of her history, she has taken directly opposite sides of the great moral question of the slave trade, changing her opinion to suit the selfish interest of her ruling class.

When Sir John Hawkins, in 1561, first engrafted upon English commerce the African slave trade, boasting that in providing his first slave cargo, he burnt a city of 8,000 inhabitants that he might capture 250 of them for slaves to freight his vessel, English public sentiment, so far from being shocked, not only acquiesced in the deed, but Queen Elizabeth herself openly protected, and shared in the profits of the next expedition, the success of which opened the way to England for a continued slave commerce of immense profits for 240 years. It was another English queen at a later date, Queen Anne, who gave directions to the Colonial Governor of New York " to take care that *the Almighty be devoutly and duly served,* according to the rites of the Church of England, and to give all possible encouragement to trade and traders, *particularly to the Royal African Company of England,*" which company was expressly enjoined by the queen, " to take special care that the colony should always have a *constant* and *sufficient* supply of *merchantable negroes at moderate rates.*" That a marvellous change has occurred in English sentiment since those days, is sufficiently notorious.

It is not necessary to attribute to the many excellent and truly philanthropic men who originated and consummated the abolition of the slave trade, any other than a sentiment of the highest philanthropy in the measures they set on foot to suppress this odious trade, for it was not the mere emigration or transportation of Africans to America, nor their condition of slavery, that constituted the odiousness of the system, so much as the brutal and inhuman and reckless manner in which it was carried on by Englishmen, that roused the indignation of the people of Great Britain. It was natural that in the storm of popular indignation which arose from the disgusting manner in which this trade was conducted, an indignation which at length pervaded the kingdom, very nice discrimination would not be made by the popular mind between that part of the system embraced in the simple transportation and emigration of men and women, and the cruelties unjustly and outrageously perpetrated by the conductors of that trade.

It was natural that the masses of the population should confound both emigration, and the mode of conducting it, in one indiscriminate category, and affix to the simple emigration and transportation of Africans, and their original condition of slavery, the character which belonged only to the abuses of the system. It was not the slavery of the African, but the " *horrors of the middle passage*," in other words, the savage barbarity of the British commercial marine, that, in the days of Wilberforce and Buxton and their philanthropic associates, stirred the minds of the British people to abolish the slave trade. These philanthropists made a just and proper distinction, wholly lost sight of by the fiery fanatics of this day, between the *slave trade* and the *system of slavery*. The former, through the brutality of the English traders, had become so notoriously odious, so disgustingly hateful, from the unrestrained abuses of more than two centuries, that it at length became an easy matter to excite the community to measures for its abatement; while the latter, the system of slavery, was regarded in a very undefined degree as an evil which it was hoped might eventually in some way be abandoned. Yet *immediate emancipation* was strongly and firmly opposed even by Mr. Wilberforce and his associates, and distinctly proscribed by them as a measure instigated, not by the *friends*, but by the *enemies* of the *slave trade abolition*, for the purpose of defeating that *abolition*.

Nor is it necessary to include in this censure, which Americans must pass upon the guilty authors of this intrigue in Great Britain to divide our Union, the masses of the English people, or even the *majority* of the aristocracy, who may possibly be ignorant of the settled purpose of the Exeter Hall or Stafford House portion of the latter class, who for their own selfish ends may be more active and prominent in the intrigue; and even if cognizant of the intrigue of certain aristocratic coteries, may be induced silently to acquiesce, without critically scrutinizing the moral aspects of the intrigue, since its political purpose on the whole is favorable to the power of their caste. Selfishness evinced in the individual is condemned as a mean and unworthy passion, but diffused through a mass, beginning with the smaller, and gradually increasing to larger associations, a family, a state or a nation, it passes in its moral aspect from being considered a low passion, to take the complexion even of a virtue. Hence bodies of men do acts, and encourage measures, of which, in their individual position, they would be heartily ashamed. No one who has studied the clannish character of the British aristocracy can have failed to observe that the strength, the well-being, the security of its caste, has to it the force of a moral law, and the conscience of its members is as sensitive to any infraction of its stability, as the individual conscience is to a law of God. Hence all the intrigues to sow divisions among other nations, where by such acts it is possible to add to the power and stability of their caste, however base and profligate and atrocious, are pursued without a single conscientious self-reproach. The fleet of a friendly neighbor, confidingly lying dismantled in its own harbor, is ruthlessly and insultingly seized on the plea that self-protection required the act. Commanding points throughout the world are seized on any plausible pretext, in order that the British maritime supremacy, directly and intimately connected with the power of the aristocracy, may be secured and extended. India is to be sub-dued that its wealth may be controlled and be poured into the lap of the aristocracy, to sustain its life and feed its power. China is invaded for the same purpose. Intrigues to foment divisions between rival parties are rife throughout India, and Britain takes part with that party, utterly reckless of its moral merits, which best promises her the control of both. The local and humane laws of these countries are superciliously set at naught by her, and the nauseous drug that stupefies and kills its millions per annum, the drug benevolently forbidden by the more conservative and more truly humane, though heathen Chinaman, is forced upon a population that would, but for British cupidity, reject it with loathing; but the law of self-preservation and well-being utters its commands, and the Chinese are condemned to a slow and idiotic death, that the coffers of the British aristocracy may be filled with these wages of iniquity.

But Britain boasts of her Christian civilization, and indeed were it not that the salt of a genuine Christianity, mixed indeed with much of human infirmity, truly permeates enough of her population to stay the doom of Sodom, we might expect to see that doom executed any moment. If, while individual sins re-ceive their punishment in a future life, national sins are punished in this life, the largest charity cannot but see in a not far distant future, a terrible retribution for that guilty Government.

B.

THE PRESENT ATTEMPT TO DISSOLVE THE AMERICAN UNION, A BRITISH ARISTOCRATIC PLOT.

———•••———

THE following important letter was written by Sidney E. Morse, Esq., and published (Dec., 1860) in *Harper's Weekly*. The writer is well known as a gentleman of intelligence and integrity, and just now this letter has a fearful significance. When it was published, more than a year ago, the anti-slavery press ridiculed it and sneered at it; but just now, perhaps, their eyes are sufficiently opened to see what tools they have been in the hands of the British aristocracy :—

A VIEW BEHIND THE CURTAIN.

In the Fall of 1853 the writer met in Paris the late Mr. Aaron Leggett, formerly a wealthy merchant in this city, and a member of the Society of Friends. We conversed frequently on the political prospects of our country as affected by the agitation of the slavery question. Mr. L. said that, when he was a young man, he was an active and zealous member of a Manumission society, and that he continued to cherish in after life a very compassionate feeling for the poor negroes. At the time of the general emancipation of the slaves in the British West Indies, Mr. Leggett's business called him to the city of Mexico, and while residing there he met Deputy Commissary-General Wilson, of the British army, an agent appointed by the British Government to make the financial arrangements connected with the payment to the West India slaveholders of their portion of the £20,000,000 voted by the British Parliament as a compensation for the forced sacrifice of their property.

Mr. Leggett said that, when he learned Mr. Wilson's errand,

he took occasion, while he was sitting with him one day after dinner, to express his admiration of the British Government and the British people, for that noble act, the vote of £20,000,000 sterling, to procure liberty for 800,000 negroes! He gave full utterance to his feelings, and almost exhausted the vocabulary of eulogy to find the commendatory epithets which he applied to England and Englishmen.

"Mr. Wilson did not seem to sympathize with me," said Mr. L., "and when I had finished, he turned to me and said, '*Do you think, Mr. Leggett, that this emancipation of the negroes will prove to be a wise measure?*'"

"Certainly, I replied," said Mr. L. "How can it be otherwise?"

"The cool heads in England," said Mr. Wilson, "do not think that it will be beneficial in its effects on the interests of the people either in its colonies or in the mother country. Nor do I think so. *We think that the freed negroes will do very little work; and that the West India Colonies, as to their commercial value to the mother country, will be ruined.*"

Mr. Leggett had been carried away with representations of the enthusiastic friends of emancipation—that free labor was more productive than slave labor; that when the negroes were free they would receive wages, and that this would stimulate them to raise sugar and coffee in greater quantities; that commerce would feel the benefit of the new impulse to agriculture; that lands would rise in value; that the income of the planters would be increased, &c.; and his ardor was at first cooled by Mr. Wilson's gloomy view of the case.

"After a little reflection, however," said Mr. L., "I continued my eulogy of the British Government and the British people; and I went now further than before in the expressions of my admiration, but I went on a new tack. I said that the enemies of Englishmen, and of their Government, were accustomed to represent them as always governed by mercenary considerations, and too willing to sacrifice justice, humanity, and all the virtues, to the lust of gain; but here was a case in which the cool heads that directed the action of the Government deliberately burdened their country with an immense debt, not to open new fields of wealth, but in full prospect of destroying the commercial value of their West India colonies, and of impoverishing the people there, and the proprietors in England—and all from a humane feeling, and a high sense of justice—a high sense of what is due to poor, helpless, down-trodden negro slaves. It was the noblest act recorded in history! I knew of no parallel to it anywhere."

"When I had finished," added Mr. L., "Mr. W. again turned to me, and said: '_Mr. Leggett, do you really believe that the men who control the action of the British Government were led by such motives as you ascribe to them, to sacrifice the commercial interests of their country?_'"

"I replied," said Mr. L., "that if the men who controlled the action of the British Government really believed that the abolition of slavery in the British West Indies would end in the commercial ruin of the islands, I could not conceive of any other motive for their conduct than the noble one which I had assigned."

"Well, Mr. Leggett," said Mr. W., "you may believe this, but I do not. I believe that the action of the British Government is made to promote, as far as possible, the INTERESTS of the English aristocracy."

Mr. L. then asked, "What interest of the English aristocracy will be promoted by the ruin of the British West India islands?"

Mr. Wilson said that the abolition of slavery in the British colonies would naturally create an enthusiastic anti-slavery sentiment in England and America, and that in America this would in process of time excite a hostility between the free States and the slave States, which would end in a dissolution of the American Union, and the consequent failure of the grand experiment of democratic government; and the ruin of Democracy in America would be the perpetuation of aristocracy in England. I do not undertake to give the language of Mr. Leggett, but the following paraphrase conveys, in my own language, the impression made upon my mind of the course of reasoning by which Mr. W. came to his conclusion:

"The English aristocracy have ruled England for ages. Their position is more enviable than that of any similar class in any other country on the globe. They rule the wealthiest empire in the world. Their landed estates embrace a large portion of all the lands in the kingdom; and these estates are entailed in their families. The House of Lords is composed exclusively of the aristocracy; and they have such influence in the elections that the members of the House of Commons are to a great extent the near relatives of the Lords. Offices of honor and power, and sinecure offices with large incomes, in the church, the army, the navy, the colonies, at foreign courts, and in all the departments of home government, are in their gift, and can be bestowed at their pleasure upon their relatives and friends. They have inherited these privileges from their ancestors, and their great aim, their ruling desire, is to retain them in their families, and to transmit them to their posterity. Their control of the public press, and of all the fountains of popular opinion and sentiment in England, has enabled them to impress the minds of the great body of the middle classes there with the belief that the English aristocracy, with its powers and privileges, is essential to the prosperity and glory of the English nation.

" Recently, however, this belief has been seriously shaken by the success of Democratic institutions in America. Englishmen are getting now to be well acquainted with America; and they see there a people of the same race with themselves, speaking the same language, reading the same books, holding the same religious opinions, loving the same pursuits; in short, like themselves in every respect except that they have no aristocracy; and yet, under their Democratic institutions, Americans are advancing even more rapidly than Englishmen, in commerce and the arts, in the diffusion of knowledge among the people, in population, wealth, and all the elements of national greatness; and intelligent men of the middle classes in England are beginning to think that aristocracy, with its heavy taxation for the support of sinecure offices, may not be so essential as they have heretofore supposed to the prosperity of England; and that the English people would, perhaps, make more rapid progress if they should throw off this burden, by Republicanizing or Americanizing their institutions. The great danger to the English aristocracy lies in this idea in the minds of the English people; for if it should take root and spread, it might end in a revolution in which they would lose all their privileges. Hence they study every thing in America and in England with the deepest interest in its bearings on this matter.

" The English aristocracy know that the English people are a liberty-loving, a liberty-vaunting people. They saw with what ease numerously-signed petitions for the abolition of slavery could be obtained in districts, and among classes, where was *no interest* to check the current of the popular feeling. *They knew that they could have found no difficulty in disposing of such petitions in Parliament without granting them, for they could have continued to receive them respectfully, and postpone action upon them endlessly, if their interest had required it.* But after a time they, doubtless, reasoned with themselves thus :

" What will be the effect of encouraging and finally granting these petitions ? If slavery shall be abolished in the British colonies, by compensating slaveholders for their losses, nobody in England will then have any interest in opposing the wildest and most enthusiastic expressions of anti-slavery sentiment. Englishmen will then love to refer with pride and boasting to the large sum sacrificed by their Government, with their concurrence, on the altar of liberty, justice, and humanity. They will then look to America, and they will see slavery still there, for Southern slaveholders in America, of course, will never ruin themselves and their country by imitating Great Britain in abolishing it. Englishmen can then be easily excited, on account of American slavery, to look down with scorn upon Americans and American institutions ; and if any popular orator, or writer, in England shall propose to deprive the aristocracy of their powers and privileges, and to fortify his argument shall refer to the prosperity of America under democratic institutions, he will be met with this scorn and defeated in his purpose.

" This will be the effect in England of the abolition of slavery in the British colonies; but the most important effect will be the effect in America. America is divided almost equally between free States and slave States—between States in which the negroes are so few that no harm results from their emancipation, and States in which slavery is so deeply rooted that it cannot be safely abolished without ruin to all classes of the population. In the free States a fierce anti-slavery sentiment, a bitter hatred of slavery and slaveholders can be excited almost as easily as in England, and in process of time, by constantly fanning the flame, such a hostility can be kindled between the people of the two great sections that it will lead to the destruction of the American Union, and the failure of the grand experiment of democratic government by men of the Anglo-Saxon race. And this failure of democracy in America will be a new lease, and a long lease, to the English aristocracy of their powers and privileges. In short, Mr. Leggett, *I believe that the English aristocracy lent their influence to the abolition of slavery in the British colonies that they may use it as a wedge for the division of the American Union.*

" *They did it to promote their own interest, to perpetuate their own privileges, by the destruction of the Union and the prosperity of Democratic America ; and to secure their object, they care no more for a debt of £20,000,000 sterling and the commercial ruin of the British West India Islands, than for the ashes of that cigar you are smoking.*"

In the above sketch, I repeat, I do not profess to give the language of Mr. L., but have endeavored, in my own language, to convey the impression made upon my mind of the course of reasoning by which Mr. W. came to his conclusion. The words in italics, however, are very nearly the words used by Mr. Leggett.

What struck me as particularly noteworthy in Mr. Leggett's narrative was, that *before the experiment of negro emancipation in the British West Indies had been fully tried, and while the friends and supporters of the measure professed to believe that its effects would be happy upon those immediately connected with it, both in the islands and in England, an agent of the British Government, who must have had uncommon opportunities for forming a sound judgment in the case, expresses his belief that they who controlled the action of the Government knew, when they gave their sanction to the measure, that there was every reason to expect that it would be calamitous to the negroes, to the planters, and to the British people, and knew, too, that they could easily have prevented it, but that they still supported and encouraged it, because it would promote the interest of the English aristocracy, by enabling them to excite in the free States of America such an anti-slavery feeling as would lead to a division of the American Union and the destruction of the great Democratic Republic.*

A constant attendance at the meetings of religious and philanthropic societies, and especially of anti-slavery meetings, during a residence of four years in London, thoroughly satisfied me that anti-slavery meetings and excitements are got up in England, not for the purpose of a removal or an amelioration of the evils of slavery in any part of the world, but chiefly, if not exclusively, with a view to keep up in the hearts of the English people a hatred of the people and institutions of America.

And as to our own country, all who are acquainted with the history of the anti-slavery movement here, know that, prior to the abolition of slavery in the British colonies, the American anti-slavery sentiment was eminently kind, considerate, rational, and Christian; that it had already happily effected the gradual abolition of slavery in all the Northern States, and was at the time very active in the border Slave States, especially among the slaveholders, who, after individually emancipating scores of thousands of their own slaves, united with each other in anti-slavery societies to promote the gradual, but eventually total, abolition of slavery by law in their respective States, with fair prospects of success in Delaware, Maryland, Virginia, Kentucky, and Missouri, and with some hope even in North Carolina and Tennessee—the emancipation of the slaves in most of these States to go hand in hand with their removal to other lands. It is also well known, that immediately after the abolition of slavery in the British colonies, anti-slavery societies of a totally different character were formed in New England, and that these societies were based on the principles of bitter hatred to all slaveholders, and a fierce denunciation of the measures which had been framed with great consideration and wisdom by Southern slaveholders, for the welfare of their slaves, and the elevation of the negro race. It is known that the supporters of these New England anti-slavery societies established newspapers, and issued tracts, employed lecturers, and devised plans, evidently intended to irritate Southern men, and provoke to acts which would irritate Northern men, and provoke retaliatory acts, and thus by continued angry action and reaction, ripen a hostility between the North and the South, which would naturally end in a dissolution of the American Union. This system of hostility has been kept up now for twenty-five years, and, with what effect, let the present state of the country answer.

How much of the large amount of money expended by American Abolitionists in support of this organized system of hostility to the Constitution of the United States, has been contributed in England, we know not, but we do know that, while conservative Americans have often been publicly and wantonly insulted in England in connection with the slavery question, and without apology, where apology was due, from members of the aristocracy, other Americans, whose chief claim to notice was the zeal and success with which they had attacked a fundamental law of their country and promoted bitter strife between the people of its two great sections, have been invited to the homes of the English nobility, flattered, honored, and encouraged on their return to America to renew their warfare upon the people and institutions of the South. These facts are readily explained on the theory of Deputy Commissary-General Wilson, that the aim of the English aristocracy is to perpetuate their own power and privileges by destroying the great American Democratic Republic, and they cannot, we think, be satisfactorily explained on any other theory.

Sidney E. Morse.

For the Journal of Commerce.

IS THE DISSOLUTION OF THE UNION THE CONSUMMATION OF A WELL DEVISED BRITISH PLOT?

Messrs. Editors:—Many think so; and there is more evidence of the truth of an affirmative answer to this pregnant question than superficial observers are probably aware.

If calm, sober, thinking men, north and south, would but carefully consider whether they have not been the dupes of a subtle foreign intrigue, it would seem that a great change in their reciprocal feelings might be the result. There is evidence if they will but search for it, and well weigh it, to make very palpable how gradually and artfully these designs have for years been in progress, till the end aimed at is at length accomplished: the Union is divided, and civil war begun.

Many of your readers will have doubtless perused an article in *Harper's Weekly* of Dec. 15, 1860, written by Sidney E. Morse, Esq., late editor of the *Observer*, giving some singular facts on this very subject, which drew forth a disparaging article in the *Tribune*, pronouncing the revelations there made "a hoax." In that article Mr. Morse gives, under his own name, a statement of a conversation in Paris with a gentleman, the late Aaron Leggett, Esq., well known in this community, not long since deceased, a gentleman of great benevolence of heart, but, like most of his creed of the "Society of Friends," carried away in his views on slavery by a mistaken philanthropy. Mr. Leggett gives clearly and consistently to Mr. Morse the conversations he had held with a distinguished British official in Mexico, Deputy Commissary-General Wilson, a gentleman who, from his position, would not be likely to misrepresent the opinions of his principals, nor would Mr. Leggett, who was an enthusiast on the subject of abolishing slavery, be likely to mis-state to Mr. Morse the uttered sentiments of a British officer, whose revelations naturally roused his own patriotism in antagonism to his cherished philanthropic design, and brought them in conflict with each other. There are in the circumstances of the case, therefore, nothing which can create a suspicion of dishonesty in any of the parties concerned, but on the contrary, every thing which entitles their statements to be received as true. If doubt be raised in the minds of any, the cause is not in the statement of Mr. Morse, nor in the statement of Mr. Leggett; it must rest solely in the statement of General Wilson, and the probabilities of the truth of his views and reasoning will receive confirmation or refutation from other sources. The subject is of too much importance to be dismissed with a sneer or indecent personalities.

Whether the fierce and reckless sectional strife that has been kept up for five and twenty years throughout our land, is the natural result of our own professed progress in enlightenment, or has been fanned and fed by foreign intrigue for deep political ends, is surely a question not to be lightly treated. It certainly concerns us to know whether we are not at this moment the victims of a deeply-laid foreign scheme, for the quenching of a light which, however unconsciously to ourselves, is revealing to the European people, as we have believed, the unsound parts of their governmental systems.

Are, indeed, the revelations of Commissary-General Wilson so chimerical? Have there been no other indications that the

British Government has not merely indirectly fed the slavery agitation in this country, but has zealously, persistently, and directly encouraged it in every possible way? Need we more than allude to the mission of a Member of Parliament, who, as an abolition lecturer, filled the country for a season with excitement, and strengthened, if he did not initiate, the wicked system of crimination and abuse of our Southern brethren? Were there no indications of foreign complicity in the John Brown raid?* Who was Colonel Forbes? What did the Stafford House junto mean in their ovations to Mrs. Beecher Stowe? Was there no political object in this movement, and in the subscriptions raised to operate against slavery in this country? Why is America on this subject to this hour insulted in the persons of any of her citizens who visit England in all circles under the influence of this aristocratic clique in Britain? Why the marked favor shown in the same circles to the most violent and unprincipled abolitionists who visit them from this side of the water? There is a political purpose at the bottom of all this, and Gen. Wilson does not stand alone in revealing what it is.

We have come into possession of an article from the highest source, published in London some time since, which very distinctly states the political object which is to be attained by the British Government through the persistent agitation of the slavery question in Great Britain and the United States, and as it is directly confirmatory, from an independent source, of Gen. Wilson's revelations, we will copy it, premising, that it will be remembered that a lady traveller from Britain, holding one of the highest positions in the Queen's household, the Hon. Amelia Murray, lady in waiting to Her Majesty, visited the United States in the

* A very calm and carefully prepared article by a Reporter of the *New York Herald*, who visited Canada for the purpose of ascertaining the condition of the colored population in Canada, thus states, previous to the secession of South Carolina: " I conversed with a prominent abolitionist in Chatham (Canada) holding a public position of trust and honor, who told me that the first suggestion of the Harper's Ferry attack was made to Brown by British abolitionists in Chatham, and who assured me that he himself subscribed money to aid Brown in raising men for the service in Ohio and elsewhere in the States. That he and his associates looked with expectation and hope to the day, not far distant, when a *disruption of the Union* would take place."

year 1854, travelling extensively at the South as well as the North. She examined the condition of African slavery at the South, and on her return to England, she published her letters, in which she honestly gives her convictions that American Slavery had been wholly misconceived and misunderstood by the Stafford House junto, since, from her own experience in the United States, she was persuaded that the actual status of slavery there had been grossly misrepresented. Much excitement was created at Court by Miss Murray's letters, and she was at once dismissed from her position near the Queen. This act on the part of the Queen's advisers created a feeling of indignation in certain quarters, and Miss Murray had many sympathizers as one persecuted for honest opinion's sake, and for telling the truth. This state of feeling made it necessary to give some explanation to the public, and the following article was published in the London *Athenæum* of January 26th, 1856, at page 107, bearing intrinsic evidence of its emanation from a source near the throne :

"A paragraph is passing round the papers in which the names of the Queen and her lady-in-waiting, the Hon. Miss Murray, are introduced, containing some statements which are not quite true. Miss Murray, whose efforts in behalf of ragged schools, female emigration, and other philanthropic movements, have been zealous and constant, has lately been in the United States.

"While there she wrote a number of pleasant and graphic letters to her friends in London, chiefly to Lady Byron.

"These letters she has published, as the reader will see in our review columns, under the title of 'Letters from the United States, Cuba, and Canada.'

"In the course of her travels in the South Miss Murray's views of the Slavery question began to change, and at the end of fifteen months' experience of America, she felt convinced that Stafford House had closed its eyes to one side of the question. This change of view Miss Murray communicated to the Queen, who replied to her lady-in-waiting, if we are rightly informed, by some very wise and womanly counsels. Unhappily, the royal letter missed its object, and before Miss Murray had the advantage of reading her august friend's advice, she had pledged herself *not* to observe that discreet silence on a most intricate and vexed problem, which is necessary in persons holding public situations.

"Miss Murray has the courage of her opinions ; but as she chose to take a part in a discussion *that every day threatened* TO REND THE UNION, her retirement from the Queen's household follows naturally. These are the simple facts. There was no intention to dedicate the book to Her Majesty. Her Majesty never saw the proof-sheets.

" We cannot suppose that the Queen meant to rebuke Miss Murray, as the paragraph makes her, for forming an honest opinion.

" Miss Murray's retirement from the Court must be *assigned to a* POLITICAL, not a personal, motive. We see nothing in it save what is creditable alike to sovereign and subject."

This extract from a London journal of the highest character is no ordinary newspaper paragraph. It bears internal evidence of its origin directly from head-quarters, and must have the weight of a *quasi-official* document.

It is not possible to mistake its meaning nor its significant bearing upon the long-settled purpose of Great Britain, in fanning the flame of this diabolical Abolition frenzy both in Britain and America. A great *measure of State policy* is directly named, which its inaugurators guard with the utmost jealousy. It is a measure which must be carried through reckless of truth. Romance, exaggeration, falsehood, are all pressed into the service of this Stafford House scheme, and truth of course must not flash its fatal light upon these satanic workings. Miss Murray, in her honesty, dared to tell the truth, so she must be taunted with the " courage of her opinion." She must be deposed from her position near the Queen lest the truth might fatally reach the ears of her truth-loving sovereign ; her letters are to be ignored in the same number of the Athenæum by the shallow disparagement of a sycophantic critic, and all this lest Stafford House should be thwarted in its plan of " *rending the Union.*"

The writer uses a cautious phraseology to salve over the act of dismissal of Miss Murray, an act that was beginning to excite remarks in the English journals, remarks threatening to compromise even the Queen herself. It was a delicate task to defend Her Majesty from imputations of an arbitrary harshness in discharging Miss Murray, and at the same time to avoid denouncing her lady-in-waiting in such terms as not to arouse public sympathy in her behalf as one persecuted for opinion's sake. It must be done in a way to satisfy all parties. The writer has adroitly accomplished this part of his task, but it has been at the expense of *disclosing the secret of the Stafford House camarilla.*

The unpardonable sin of Miss Murray—the crime for which she was summarily discharged from the service of the Queen, was the venturing to hint, in the expressive language of the Athenæum, that "Stafford House had shut its eyes to one side of the question" of slavery abolition, and so she had interfered to thwart the State policy that was being pursued of "rending the Union," which project was on the point of consummation—a consummation even then looked for "every day." Can any one doubt, if Miss Murray had been weak and dishonest enough to have added fresh slanders against Southern society, professedly from her own observation, that she would have been rebuked and dismissed, for "not observing a discreet silence on this most intricate and vexed problem"?

And now in view of these facts, is it not time that the scales should drop from the eyes of our people throughout the land, that they comprehend the reality of the fatal trap into which they are hurrying in their blindness?

We beseech them, by all the sacred memories of the past, to pause *now* before the door has been irretrievably shut down, and this foreign intrigue actually consummated, and calmly reflect whither they are going. Is patriotism wholly dead? have we been indeed left to the just punishment of our national sins, and given over to the rule of passionate, obstinate, furious demagogues?

Where are the *people?* why do they sleep when incendiaries have fired the house? Why has it been that the denouement of this plot of foreign intrigue should be necessary to wake us to a sense of its actual existence?

We have been accustomed to boast that foreign arms could not subjugate us, and while a *united* people, (united *not by force* but by mutual respect and affection,) our boast (under God) is true. Nor will any foreign power attempt it upon a *united* people, but "*divide et impera*," the favorite artifice of despots, discarded to-day by glorious Italy, is practised upon with success here, (with shame be it spoken,) and America in her madness succumbs.

A few more steps urged on by the wicked fanaticism of the day, and *Ichabod* may be written across the blue field of our national standard, and then—no eye but God's can foresee the future. "*Carthago delenda est*," will be the ecstatic shout of Stafford House, and our light is quenched forever.   B.

Since the above was written, (more than *nine months* ago,)

we have noticed the recent remarks of a distinguished member of the British aristocracy, who does not hesitate to avow the very design which has been charged upon the British Government; and when we consider that this member of the House of Peers, the Earl of Shaftesbury, one of the Stafford House clique, the President of the British and Foreign Bible Society, is the same nobleman who presided at the meeting of British Abolitionists in London in July last, convened to present a piece of plate to the notorious Dr. Cheever for his efficient labors in fanning the abolition excitement in this country, and thus directly contributing to the consummation of this *now avowed* political design of Great Britain, " *of rending the Union*," it would seem that further proof was not needed.

The Earl of Shaftesbury is reported to have said to a gentleman conversing with him on American affairs :

" I, in common with almost every English statesman, *sincerely desire the rupture of the American Union*. It has been the policy of England to brook no rivalry, especially in the direction of her own greatness. We justly fear the commerical and political rivalry of the United States. With a population of thirty millions, they will soon, if *not checked*, overshadow Great Britain. We cannot look upon such a monstrous growth without apprehension."*

True words ! my lord, you have epitomized with great precision and conciseness the inner political workings of the British aristocratic mind for many long years. As a political end, *the destruction of a rival*, this end to be attained regardless of any other principle, moral or political, than *the material glory of England*, or rather, of *the British aristocracy*, " the rupture of the American Union" was a measure wisely adapted to that end, and the means adroitly chosen to destroy your trans-Atlantic rival ; but while we accord wisdom in the choice of means for destroying us, to those who are jealous of our growing strength, what shall we say of you, countrymen, North and South, who find yourselves caught in this foreign snare ? If shame can lead to repentance, if it can calm the raging of this horrible fratricidal war, and lead each section to lay down its arms under the influence of a common indignation, against a common enemy, who

---

* See Note A at the end of the pamphlet.

has deceived us both, we may yet attain to union, and to strength again, better guarded than ever heretofore, against the wiles of foreign duplicity. Shall it be done ?

For the Journal of Commerce.

THE DISSOLUTION OF THE UNION THE OBJECT OF BRITISH INTRIGUES.

In my communication published in your journal of January 13th, I gave your readers evidence which I considered conclusive, that the *dissolution of the Union* was the consummation of a well-devised plot by Great Britain, through the agitation of the slavery question. I well know that such an announcement startled many minds, and some incredulity has been manifested, notwithstanding the strength of the evidence of its truth. If further evidence is needed, let me now adduce it from the antecedents of British policy. There are official documents in the department of State deposited there fifty years ago, which every citizen would do well to review. The subject of *British intrigues* was made the occasion of a special Message by President Madison on the 9th of March, 1812, three months before the declaration of war. Your readers desirous of seeing these documents in full will find them in Benton's "Abridgment of the Debates of Congress," vol. iv., from page 506 onward.

It seems that in the year 1809, an emissary of the British Government, John Henry, a gentleman of education and address, was sent to Boston under the sanction of the Governor-General of Canada, Sir James Craig, sustained by the Home Government, by Lord Liverpool, Robert Peel, Sir George Prevost and others, for the purpose of taking advantage of the high party excitement between Federalists and Democrats at that time, for the purpose (in the language of President Madison) " of fomenting disaffection," and " destroying the Union " and " forming the eastern part thereof into a political connection with Great Britain." Although his mission was unsuccessful, because, as he himself stated, " he found it an unpopular topic," his letters demonstrate with a clearness which cannot be questioned, the settled intent of the British Government, at that early day, to *divide the Union*, as a measure deemed of the greatest importance and advantage to British interests. His correspondence shows that he faithfully carried out his instructions, but as success did not attend his efforts, the promised reward (a lucrative office) was withheld from him. Piqued at receiving the *cold shoulder* from the British officials whom he had served, he sought his revenge by revealing the plot to our Government, putting into the hands of the Secretary of State his correspondence with the British Government. With the character of the whole transaction—with its morality or immorality; with Henry's motives for betraying the confidence reposed in him ; with its success or ill success, or with its implications upon any persons or parties of that date, we have now nothing to do; they are all matters which may be left out of consideration, as they do not affect the reality of the one great fact which these documents establish. This great fact stands out clear and prominent, that Great Britain did at that day employ an emissary to foment disaffection in the country, and this for the purpose of *dividing the Union.* A few extracts from Henry's letters will demonstrate this fact beyond dispute. On his way to Boston, writing from Burlington, Vt., Feb. 14, 1809, Henry says : " In what mode this resistance (to the Administration) will first show itself is probably not yet determined upon ; and may, in some measure, depend upon the reliance that the leading men may place upon *assurances of support from his Majesty's representatives in Canada ; and as I shall be on the spot to tender this, whenever the moment arrives that it can be done with effect,* there is no doubt that all their measures may be made subordinate to the intentions of his Majesty's Government. Great pains are taken by the men of talent and intelligence to confirm the fears of the common people, as to the concurrence of the Southern Democrats in the projects of France ; *and every thing tends to encourage the belief that the* Dissolution *of the* Confederacy *will be accelerated* by the spirit which now actuates both political parties."

In a letter dated Boston, March 7, 1809, Henry says : " What permanent connection between Great Britain and this section of the Republic would grow out of a civil commotion, such as might be expected, no person is prepared to describe ; but it seems that a strict alliance must result of necessity. At present the opposition party confine their calculations merely to resistance, and I can assure you that, at this moment, they do not freely entertain *the project of withdrawing the Eastern States from the Union, finding it a very unpopular topic ;* although a course of events, such as I have already mentioned, *would inevitably produce an incurable alienation of the New England from the Southern States.*"

Again, in a letter dated Boston, March 9, 1809 : " The Government of the United States would probably complain, and Bonaparte become peremptory ; but even that would only tend to render the opposition in the Northern States more resolute, and *accelerate the dissolution of the Confederacy.*"

In a letter dated Boston, March 13, 1809, he says : " Bonaparte, whose passions are too hot for delay, will probably compel this Government to decide which of the two great belligerents is to be its enemy. *To bring about a separation of the States, under distinct and separate Governments,* is an affair of more uncertainty, and, *however desirable,* cannot be effected BUT BY A SERIES OF ACTS AND A LONG-CONTINUED POLICY TENDING TO IRRITATE THE SOUTHERN AND CONCILIATE THE NORTHERN PEOPLE. The former are agricultural, the latter a commercial people. The mode of cherishing and depressing either is too obvious to require illustration. *This, I am aware, is an object of much interest in Great Britain,* as it would forever secure the integrity of his Majesty's possessions on this continent, and *make the two Governments,* or whatever number the present confederacy might form into, *as much subject to the influence of Great Britain as her colonies can be rendered.* But it is an object only to be attained by *slow and circumspect progression,* and requires *for its consummation more attention* to the affairs which agitate and excite parties in this country, *than Great Britain has yet bestowed upon it.* I lament the repeal of the embargo, *because it was calculated to accelerate the progress of these States towards a revolution that would have put an end to* the only republic that remains to prove that a government founded on political equality can exist in a season of trial and difficulty, or is calculated to insure either security or happiness to a people."

In a letter, March 29, 1809, he says :

" It should, therefore, be the *peculiar care* of Great Britain *to foster divisions between the North and the South,* and by succeeding in this, she may carry into effect her own projects in Europe, with a total disregard of the Democrats of this country."

On May 5th, 1809, he commences his letter thus:

"Although the recent changes that have occurred quiet all apprehensions of war, *and consequently lessen all hope of a separation of the States,*" &c.

Enough has been quoted to substantiate the fact that the deliberate design of Great Britain fifty years ago was to foment divisions between the two geographical sections of the country, in order to effect a special purpose, and that purpose the *dissolution of the Union.*

If it be asked how was the development of this plot received by the Government? a quotation or two from the speeches in Congress upon this topic will show.

Mr. Gholson, of Virginia, said: "This communication," from the President, "demonstrated as matter of fact, what had heretofore remained only speculation and conjecture, *that the British Government has long meditated* THE SEPARATION OF THESE STATES; and what is more, that they have actually attempted the execution of this wicked design, and have endeavored *to convert our own citizens into traitors.*"

Mr. Troup, of Georgia, said: "The documents have a most important bearing. They establish the fact that a foreign Government, on the eve of hostility with us, has for some time past employed an agent to foment division among us; and another fact, which, considered in connection with other circumstances, is of great importance. They show the deep-rooted hostility of this foreign Power to our Republican Government and liberties— *a hostility which could stop at nothing short of a* DISMEMBERMENT OF THE COUNTRY."

Mr. Fisk, of Vermont, said: "Why, sir, can gentlemen seriously doubt the truth of the facts stated by this Mr. Henry, when they have it from the highest authority that the former British Minister, Mr. Erskine, while here, at this very time, was in the same business this Henry was sent to perform?" Mr. Fisk then quotes an official letter from Mr. Erskine to his Government, dated Feb. 15, 1809: "The ultimate consequences of such differences and jealousies, arising between the Eastern and Southern States, would inevitably tend to a *dissolution of the Union,* which has been for *some time talked of*, and has of late, as I have heard, been seriously contemplated by many of the leading people of the Eastern division."

Mr. Macon, the veteran statesman of North Carolina, said : " Nothing can be more true than that these papers do prove that Great Britain has not yet ceased her attempts to disturb the peace of this nation." "As to this man, he is just such an one as the British usually employ for these purposes; he is one of their own agents." "The question is, Has he told the truth ? I verily believe he has. I understood enough of the papers, as read, to know that he was the Agent of the British Government, *sent here to sow dissension*, and that was enough for me. So long as we are governed by interest, mutual wants, or common sense, *so long shall we continue united*. We are placed in such a situation that we ought to love each other, *and we always should, did not mad passions* sometimes run away with us." "We supply each other's wants; *we ought* never to dream of separation. And when these messengers of hell are sent here shall we not look at them ? "

No comment can present the fact in a stronger light, that Great Britain seriously determined, by fomenting dissensions in the country, to *dissolve the Union of the States*, at that date of our history. Foiled in her attempts then, and with the same, if not a greater interest to consummate the same project, is it reasonable to suppose she has abandoned it, or is it not much more reasonable to conclude that she will attempt to compass her ends by other means ? It is the maxim of a profound statesman of the last age—Lord Shelburn—that "in politics none must have a *power* joined to an *interest* to do mischief, whatever be the purity of their original intentions." We may adopt the maxim with profit, and leave out altogether the qualification of "purity of original intentions." The subject is prolific of thought, and is commended to the reflection of every truly American heart from Maine to the Rio Grande.   B.

The " disclaimer " referred to in the following communication, is disposed of by our correspondent B., to whom we have shown the article, as our readers will perceive in the present number of our journal.—*Editor Journal of Commerce.*

For the Journal of Commerce.

BRITISH INTRIGUES TO DISSOLVE THE UNION.

MESSRS. EDITORS:—Your correspondent B. in your issue of 3d inst. has given certain extracts from the correspondence and disclosures of Capt. John Henry, in 1809, to show that the British Government at that time were intent on separating the United States. So far as this dishonorable man is concerned, it only shows that he was desirous of such an issue to secure to himself the rewards of a spy. Your correspondent in fairness ought to have stated that the British Government through its Minister at Washington promptly disavowed any complicity in the transaction. On the 11th of March the British Minister, Mr. Foster, sent to the Secretary of State the following disclaimer, which was transmitted to Congress by Mr. Madison two days after, and thus settled the matter.

WASHINGTON, *March* 11, 1812.

The undersigned, his Britannic Majesty's Envoy Extraordinary and Minister Plenipotentiary to the United States, has read in the public papers of this city, with the deepest concern, the Message sent by the President of the United States to Congress on the 9th instant, and the documents which accompanied it. In the utter ignorance of the undersigned as to all the circumstances alluded to in those documents he can only disclaim most solemnly, on his own part, the having had any knowledge whatever of the existence of such a mission or of such transactions as the communication of Mr. Henry refers to, and express his conviction that from what he knows of those branches of his Majesty's Government with which he is in the habit of having intercourse, no countenance whatever was given by them to any schemes hostile to the internal tranquillity of the United States. The undersigned, however, cannot but trust that the American Government and the Congress of the United States will take into consideration the character of the individual who has made the communication in question, and will suspend any further judgment on its merits until the circumstances shall have been made known to his Majesty's Government. The undersigned requests the Secretary of State to accept the assurances of his highest consideration. [Signed]　　　　AUGUSTUS J. FOSTER.

Respectfully,

ANGLICUS.

For the Journal of Commerce.

THE DISSOLUTION OF THE UNION, A PLOT OF THE BRITISH ARISTOCRACY.

MESSRS. EDITORS:—The facts given in my last communication, demonstrating from official records that the attempt was made by Great Britain in 1809 to foment divisions between the North and South, confessedly for the purpose of *Dissolving the Union*, ought to be sufficient to lead the reflecting in the country deeply to ponder the question whether we are not now the dupes of another and more successful intrigue from the same quarter. I am much obliged to your correspondent *Anglicus* for alluding to the *pretended* disclaimer of the British Government through its Minister, for he will see that *irrefutable evidence* is herein brought forward of the complicity of the British Government in that disgraceful intrigue to rend our Union. One only attempt to gainsay the facts of Henry's disclosures has ever been made, and this will need but a moment's attention to show its futility. The British Minister, Mr. Foster, as *Anglicus* has shown, did send to the Secretary of State on the 11th of March, 1812, a *Disclaimer*, in consequence of the Message of the President, of March 9th, accompanying Henry's disclosures. Were this, indeed, an official denial of the *British Government* of any participation in these disgraceful intrigues, the character of the whole transaction would have been essentially modified. But how stands the case? It is not a disclaimer of the charge against the British Government. It is a meagre document of a few lines, merely disclaiming " *on his own part* having had any *knowledge whatever* of the existence of such a mission, and expressing his conviction that from what he knows of those branches of his Majesty's Government *with whom he is in the habit of having intercourse*, no countenance was given *by them* to any schemes hostile to the internal tranquillity of the United States;" and then he " asks a suspension of judgment of its merits until the circumstances shall have been made known to his Majesty's Government." This is all that has ever been said officially by way of explanation on the part of the British Government, from that day to this. That Mr. Foster did not *personally know* of such a mission may well be conceded without affecting the truth of Mr. Henry's disclosures one iota, or disproving the complicity of the British Government in them ; and as to the *suspension of judgment* requested, till explanation should be given by his Majesty's Government, that explanation has never been made to this hour. We shall presently see what course " his Majesty's Government " pursued when the subject was brought to their notice.

But how was this matter viewed by President Madison and the Committee of Foreign Relations? If this disclaimer had any weight with them, their subsequent action will certainly show it.

Five days after the disclaimer, to wit, on March 16th, the report of the Committee of Foreign Relations, to whom was referred the President's Message of 9th of March, with these disclosures of Henry, contains the following remarks :—" It may be satisfactory to the House to be informed that the original papers, with the *evidences* relating to them in possession of the Executive, were submitted to their examination, and were such as *fully to satisfy* the Committee of their *genuineness*." And again : " The transaction disclosed by the President's Message presents to the mind of the Committee *conclusive evidence that the British Government, at a period of peace,* and *during the most friendly professions,* have been *deliberately* and *perfidiously* pursuing measures to *divide these States,* and to involve our citizens in all *the guilt of treason* and the *horrors of a civil war* —a proceeding, which at all times and among all nations, has been considered as one of the *most aggravated character,* and which *ought to be regarded by us with the deepest abhorrence.*"

It is worthy of notice that these very intrigues, to divide the Union, were set forth by the President in his Message to Congress, of June 1st, 1812, among the "*injuries* and *indignities*" which demanded the declaration of war with Great Britain in 1812; the President says : "It has since *come into proof,* that at the very moment when the public Minister was holding the language of friendship, and inspiring confidence in the sincerity of the negotiation with which he was charged, *a secret agent of his Government was employed in intrigues, having for their object a subversion of our Government,* and a DISMEMBERMENT OF OUR HAPPY UNION."

Subsequently, the Committee of Foreign Relations, (of which

Mr. Calhoun was Chairman,) to which Committee this Message was referred, thus adverts to these intrigues :—"Your Committee would be much gratified if they could close here the detail of British wrong; but it is their duty to recite another act of *still greater malignity* than any of those which have already been brought to your view. *The attempt to* DISMEMBER OUR UNION, and overthrow our excellent Constitution by a *secret mission*, the object of which was to *foment discontent and excite insurrection* against the constituted authorities and laws of the nation, *as lately disclosed by the agent employed in it*, affords full proof that there is no bounds to the hostility of the British Government towards the United States; *no act however unjustifiable, which it would not commit to accomplish their ruin.* This attempt excites the greater horror, from the consideration that it was made while the United States and Great Britain were at peace, and an amicable negotiation was depending between them for the accommodation of their differences."

The Committee, after saying "they feel no hesitation in advising resistance by force," close their report with these words : "Your Committee recommend an immediate appeal to arms;" Congress accepted this report, and the Bill declaring war against Great Britain was passed.

In compliance with the request of the British Minister that we "suspend judgment until the circumstances shall have been made known to his Majesty's Government," and for the satisfaction of your correspondent *Anglicus*, let us glance a moment at the proceedings of the British Government, when this subject of Henry's disclosures reached England.

On May 5, 1812, Lord Holland, in the House of Lords, gave notice of a motion to call for the correspondence in relation to this Intrigue. If the Government is innocent, there can be no reason for withholding the correspondence; if guilty, we look for a strenuous effort to suppress inquiry. Instead of seconding the call, there was so much fluttering in the Ministerial ranks that it became at once evident that a tender spot was touched. The Ministry vigorously opposed the motion under various trifling pretexts, while they gave a feeble disclaimer of participation in Henry's mission, endeavoring to throw the obloquy of the transaction upon the late Governor-General of Canada, Sir James

Craig, who had then but recently deceased. Lord Darnley contended that such disclaimer on the part of Government was not satisfactory; he said : " He could not but remember that this renunciation of all participation rested solely upon their assertion, while *presumptive evidence was very strong against them.*"

Lord Lauderdale said, in view of what the Ministers had advanced, " what security had the United States that there was not another Captain Henry pursuing a similar conduct in that country at this moment ? "

Lord Holland closed the debate; he said : " His whole object in making the motion was to refute the charge brought against the English Government if it could be done, and if not, to punish those with whom the guilt lay ; *but in refusing all inquiry,* they were giving the world *no answer to that charge.* They might say in that house it was partly false and partly true, but such allegation *was no solemn and authentic disavowal to America or to Europe,* and it remained, therefore, unrefuted." The House then divided ; 27 voted in favor of producing the correspondence, and 73 voted against its production, leaving a majority of 46 in favor of the ministerial attempt to hush up the matter. Every one can make his own inference on this result.   B.

For the Journal of Commerce.

THE DISSOLUTION OF THE UNION THE OBJECT OF BRITISH INTRIGUES.

Messrs. Editors :—I think I have shown beyond dispute in my former communications that one of the causes distinctly set forth by the President and by Congress for the declaration of war between Great Britain and the United States in 1812 was this dishonorable attempt on the part of the former Government, through its secret agents, to foment divisions and create irritations, between the Northern and Southern sections of the country, and this for the express purpose of *dismembering the Union.* Great Britain was directly charged with this attempt by the United States Government, and the suppression of all inquiry on the subject in the British Parliament, when the Ministry of that day were called upon by Lord Holland in the House of Peers to clear themselves from that charge, stamps forever the fact that to this day, (to use the words of Lord Holland,) " *the charge remains unrefuted.*"

With this charge, then, fully admitted and established, it becomes a matter of importance to us to inquire, 1st. Whether the results of that war were calculated to lessen or to increase the desire for the consummation of the British Aristocratic conspiracy against this country? Policy would naturally dictate both delay and caution in any measures to carry out their aim of " rending the Union " which might excite jealousy or suspicion on our part, but assuredly, the naval prowess of the Union, so strikingly prominent and so firm.ly established, by that contest, was a marked feature in the history of the war not calculated to allay the fears or the jealousies of that jealous maritime power. Is it unreasonable to suppose that the unscrupulous leaders of that proud aristocracy were fully aware of the causes of the failure of the conspiracy which they had intrusted to Henry's management? They must have become aware from the disclosures he made to them that the party differences of Federalists and Democrats, so acrimoniously contested at that period, were not of a sufficiently *Sectional* or profound a character to accomplish their policy of dividing the Union. Each of these political parties, into which the whole country was divided, had their adherents both at the North and at the South; their party differences had reference to common, not to sectional interests, and consequently a geographical or sectional division on the basis of those party differences was simply impracticable. And 2d. Were not the wise suggestions of Captain Henry—suggestions the result of his experience in his endeavors to promote their wishes—worthy of their serious consideration? He distinctly suggests to them a course for *future* operations, which we also would do well to consider, when he says to them, " To bring about a *separation of the States*, under distinct and independent governments, however desirable, cannot be effected but *by a series of acts and a long-continued* policy tending TO IRRITATE THE SOUTHERN AND CONCILIATE THE NORTHERN PEOPLE; " and again, " it is an object *only to be attained by slow and circumspect progression."*

In view of these suggestions of their agent, is it not worth while to inquire whether there are any indications of an adoption by this same jealous power of the policy thus suggested to them?

A general investing a fortress which he is intent on capturing, does not ordinarily retire because of a single repulse from an impracticable point, especially when his spies have discovered and reported to him a vulnerable point requiring only a slower and more circumspect sapping and mining.

It is, however, of little comparative importance to know whether the subsequent action of the Aristocracy to "rend the Union," was, or was not, a consequence of these sagacious suggestions of their emissary. It is of far more importance to ascertain whether a policy in exact and palpable accord with his suggestions has, or has not, for some fifty years, been in operation.

Let it be kept in mind that the main characteristic of that policy recommended as most likely to bring about "*a separation of the States,*" is "*a policy tending to* IRRITATE THE SOUTHERN *and conciliate the Northern people.*" Now, on searching the records of our history for the basis of such a policy, a *sectional* subject of such an *irritating* character as shall answer this purpose, is there one which could be found by the managers of the intrigue, better adapted to create *irritation of the South*, than the subject of African slavery?

It was a profound remark of an eminent British statesman, that "in a concern so full of duplicity as politics, *possibility* is to be regarded with as much jealousy as *certainty*, for caution will be late when opportunity for using caution is at an end." Let us then look in the direction whence this *possibility*, not to say *certainty*, may be discovered.

Not to distract by bringing to light many strong and coincident indications of the inauguration of this policy, which from the nature of the enterprise would be artfully covered up, we come at once upon an historic fact strikingly similar to Captain Henry's intrigue of 1809.

In the year 1835 there came to this country an Englishman well fitted by nature and education to inaugurate the policy of *irritation*. This man was George Thompson. He was an adept in the popular phrases of our own demagogues, possessed of that sort of eloquence which charms a certain class of shallow but excitable minds, well versed in the vocabulary of denunciation, personally proscriptive; he could talk glibly of freedom of discussion and equal rights, and fulminate bloodthirsty curses against slaveholders. He came under the cover of the Anti-Slavery Societies of Great Britain recommended to the Garrison

breed of Abolitionists. The American Anti-Slavery Society had
only two years before his advent to this country laid down the
new, unscriptural, and disastrous dogma that "all Slavery is
sin," thus giving a lever of great power for just such an emissary
as had been sent to take advantage of the dreadful mistake. So
recently had the untenable dogma been in operation when Thompson arrived, that the Anti-Slavery Societies of New England
were not yet wrought up to the degree of fanatic zeal, which in
this sad hour has culminated in our times in bloodshed and
crime ; the mass of members were yet unprepared for fully car-
rying out their new and fatal programme. The false Christian
and moral philosophy of the day had not yet sufficiently imbued
their minds, or the minds of the community at large, with the
principles of a plausible but really shallow humanitarianism, and
so the bold doctrines of this foreign emissary grated harshly even
on their ears. When he addressed them in Boston, such was his
impudent and intemperate language that there were cries of "we
want to hear no foreigners lecture us," "he has issued nothing
but one tissue of falsehoods against the South," and even one of
the delegates to the meeting from the Baptists of England was so
disgusted with Thompson's denunciations, that "he rose to express his regret at the course of remark in which he had in-
dulged." The meeting was excited, and for the most part
indignant. Wherever Thompson went throughout the country,
the same scenes followed ; the staple of his public speeches was
denunciation of the South and slaveholders ; he adhered strictly
to the programme of "*irritating the Southern people ;*" and this
end was attained by the intentional notoriety which his ultraism
gained for all that he said. He visited Theological Seminaries,
and conversed with their students to indoctrinate them in his programme of irritation. The more ultra the doctrine the more
excitement. And so to a student at Andover he distinctly de-
clares that the kind of moral instruction which ought to be en-
joyed by the slaves, was, " THAT EVERY SLAVE SHOULD BE TAUGHT
TO CUT HIS MASTER'S THROAT." When this was published, the
excitement was so great as to endanger his safety, and he did not
hesitate to deny that he had said it. The issue of that denial
was the production of irrefragable proof of his having said it, and
also of his prevarication. He became so obnoxious to the con-

servative part of the community that it was feared that violence
would be committed upon him. The Boston *Atlas* in Oct.,, 1835,
says of Thompson: "We deprecate all attempts at violence
against this individual, but we think that he has severely tried
the patience of our fellow-citizens, and done full enough to disturb the peace and good order of the community. How much
longer can we bear and forbear? A mountebank who in the ex-
ercise of his vocation should produce similar infractions of the
peace would be taken up as a vagrant, or abated as a nuisance."
About the same time, a riot in Boston was attempted in consequence of Thompson's proceedings, and was not dispersed, although the Mayor assured the mob that Thompson was not in the
city. He had fled into the country and concealed himself, while
his friend Garrison was seized and led about the streets with a
halter around his neck.

All this was making capital for Mr. Thompson's principals on
the other side of the water; the *irritating* part of the process
was in successful operation.

We need not follow the course of this emissary in the United
States further than to add a convincing proof of his success,
in conjunction with his abolition associates, in "*irritating the
Southern people*," by circulating tracts of an irritating and incendiary character at the South.

President Jackson, in his message to Congress of Dec. 7,
1835, says:—"I must also invite your attention to the painful
excitements in the South, by attempts to circulate through the
mails inflammatory appeals addressed to the passions of the slaves,
in prints and in various sorts of publications, calculated to stimulate them to insurrection, and to produce all the horrors of a ser-
vile war."   *   *   *   *   *   *

"It is fortunate for the country that the good sense, the
generous feeling, and the deep-rooted attachment of the people of
the non-slaveholding States to the Union, and their fellow-citizens
of the same blood in the South, have given so strong and impres-
sive a tone to the sentiments entertained against the proceedings
of *the misguided persons who have engaged in these unconstitu-
tional and wicked attempts, and especially against* THE EMIS-
SARIES FROM FOREIGN PARTS *who have dared to interfere in this
matter*, as to authorize the hope that *those attempts* will no

longer be persisted in. * * * I would, therefore, call the special attention of Congress to the subject, and respectfully suggest the propriety of passing such a law as will prohibit, under severe penalties, the circulation in the Southern States, through the mail, of incendiary publications intended to instigate the slaves to insurrection."

Captain Henry's efforts, in his similar but abortive effort for *dismembering the Union* in 1809, were to have been rewarded by a *Judgeship in Canada;* this we learn incidentally from the Debates in Parliament. The British Government must doubtless have felt strongly chagrined at the *faux pas* they had committed in Henry's case in not fulfilling their promises to him, and so driving him, in revenge, to divulge the whole plot to the United States Government. They were not likely to commit the same error twice, in their persistent efforts to " foment divisions " in the United States. The reward given to Mr. George Thompson for his efforts to *irritate the Southern people,* are not among the items recorded in the expenses of the Government, but the reward was nevertheless soon manifest.

In Nov., 1835, Thompson had returned to England. Let us glance a moment at his reception there. The President's Message, in which, though not named, Thompson was as clearly designated as if he had been, must have reached England about a month after Thompson's return. If Thompson's conduct in the United States was so repulsive, and so notorious as to be made the subject of a paragraph in the President's Message, it could scarcely have escaped the notice of the political community of Great Britain, and some explanation ought to have been given to the United States. Mr. Thompson, on the contrary, at once steps into the political arena, and we find him a contestant for a seat in Parliament from the Tower Hamlets. We know the influence that secures a seat in the Commons. Had Mr. Thompson's notorious course of outrage on the feelings of at least one whole section of this country and nine-tenths of the other section, been distasteful or obnoxious to the Aristocracy of Great Britain, it would have been next to impossible that he could have been elected. Nevertheless he was elected. Captain Henry stipulated for a *Judgeship in Canada,* and being refused, betrays the Conspirators. It amounts quite to demonstration that Thompson's price was *a seat in Parliament;* he performed his foreign service to the satisfaction of his. principals; for the Southern people were roused to intense indignation; and he returned home to receive his reward, an M. P. affixed to his otherwise obscure name.

Whether the demonstration we have given, that we are the dupes of a long-concocted and skilfully planned intrigue of the British aristocracy, will have any effect to allay our irritated sectional feeling, and thus dissolve the diabolical spell which keeps us from Union, is more than can now be predicted. There is food here for reflection, deep, dispassionate, serious reflection.

B.

NOTE A.

The expressions attributed to Lord Shaftesbury, on p. 22, have in substance been lately denied by that nobleman in the following note to Mr. Weed:

"FEBRUARY 20, 1862.

"DEAR MR. WEED: * * * * Be so good as to read the enclosed letter to me from Philadelphia, and then return it to me. It is one, and a sample, of many that I receive on the same subject. My reply is uniform: I have made no such speeches, attended no meeting, and have neither said nor thought any thing so foolish and mischievous as the contents of that paragraph.

"Your faithful servant,
"SHAFTESBURY."

This denial embraces several particulars, and is fruitful in important suggestions. I have no wish to deprive the noble Earl of any benefit he may personally derive from his pronouncing the sentiments attributed to him, in his alleged conversation with an American gentleman, foolish, etc. They were eminently so in every aspect, and, however ambiguous in the intended application of the term "foolish," whether folly was attributable to the idea that the aristocracy desired the dismemberment of the American Union, or, what is more in consonance with reason, attributable to the *imprudent avowal* of this well-known sentiment of that aristocracy, folly, in the sense of a violation of moral precepts, is clearly stamped on both categories.

But Lord Shaftesbury distinctly and unqualifiedly asserts that *he has attended no meeting.* Is the account, then, of the meeting held in London on the 24th of July, 1861, at which meeting Lord Shaftesbury is reported to have presided, and which was convened to present to the notorious Dr. Cheever a piece of plate, a fiction? Was it not the express purpose of that meeting to strengthen the hands and encourage the hearts of the fanatics on this side of the water, whose unchristian, misguided zeal, and infidel ravings, for some thirty years, have at length produced their natural and long-predicted fruits, to wit, a savage, relentless, bloody, fratricidal war? It is a melancholy sight to see a nobleman of such prominence as Lord Shaftesbury, carried away by the sophistry which prevails around him, lending the influence of his name and position to fan the flame of civil war in a Christian country among Christian brethren. He was chairman of the meeting, and is represented to have said, among other things, that " Englishmen had so great an idea of *individual liberty*, that it never entered into their minds *to argue the question ;* and any man expressing a doubt on the subject would be looked upon as a fool or a beast." Let us look at this plausible sophism of individual liberty, extraordinary as coming from a leading member of the English aristocracy. If individual liberty, under any and all circumstances, (for this is the unqualified assertion,) is a right so certainly true and good, it ought to be capable of clear demonstration ; *arguing the question* can do it no harm ; it should be fixed on the basis of sound reason and Scripture, and thus should not fear discussion ; above all, it should be so carefully stated as not to be liable to perversion and abuse, through any misunderstanding of its exact import, when practically applied. As stated by Lord Shaftesbury, we understand him to accept without qualification the doctrine of the American Declaration of Independence, as construed by the fanaticism of the day, that every individual man has '' an inalienable right to liberty ;" and he affirms that this is a doctrine now so well established in the English mind, that no argument on the subject pro or con would be listened to, and that any one " expressing any doubt on the subject would be esteemed a fool or a beast." This is strong language, nor ought we to doubt that Lord Shaftesbury spoke the conscientious convictions of his mind. But at the risk of being placed in the unenviable categories of a fool or a beast, I will venture to doubt the soundness of this sweeping, unqualified axiom, and also to say that the noble Earl himself will shrink from the logical results of his ill-considered postulate. And first: Do reason and common sense sanction the allowance of unqualified individual liberty to every human being ? Is the child allowed unrestricted liberty ? To uphold the axiom, as it is asserted, in its unqualified integrity, the reply must be, yes. Is his Lordship prepared to say, yes ? I will not believe that he will so unqualifiedly take this position, but, as a rational man, particularly in its logical consequences to his caste, will say that a child's liberty is of course restrained ; that every child that comes into the world is, and must of necessity be, under restraint; that, instead of being born into liberty, he is born into slavery. It is, in fact, a rule without an exception. *Slavery*, the subjection of one's will to the will of another, since the fall of man, is the rule, and not *liberty*. I speak of a fact so notorious that the " fool and beast " alone will ignore it. This great fact, that slavery since the fall is the normal condition of all mankind, lies at the basis of all government, and is recognized in the laws of every civilized nation on the globe. If the law restrains a child's liberty, and forbids his doing certain acts, until he is of age, is he not a slave to the extent of his privation of liberty until he is of age ? At the age of twenty-one he is, in common universal parlance, *free ;* what, then, was he previous to becoming of age ?

The noble Lord will not deny the facts. What say reason and common sense as to the moral character of the facts ? Is it right or is it not, that the individual should be uniformly restrained of his liberty until he is of mature age ? I must believe that Lord Shaftesbury is not prepared to abrogate the human laws that impose restraint upon minors, and for the reason that his own benevolent instincts recognize a benevolent necessity for this restraint ; it is benevolence to the child to restrain his liberty, and benevolence to society in order to protect the community against the inexperienced, heedless, or corrupt acts of an inferior portion of its members. Reason and the universal opinion and action of mankind sanction this restraint ; and when we bring the whole matter to the test of the supreme arbiter of moral controversy, the Bible, the reason for restraint is set forth in such a clear light that none but an infidel will ignore its decisions. Quotations from the Bi- ⋅ ble to sustain the authority and benevolence of restraint upon children, are certainly superfluous to the President of the British and Foreign Bible Society.

The simple fact, that the Bible not merely sanctions but enjoins subjection to authority, would of itself be sufficient to compel our assent, even if the reason of the demand were not apparent ; but in this case the reason is obvious at a glance. Man, since the fall, is a corrupt and selfish being, sensual, devoid of holiness, low and debased in his appetites, and by nature fit only for destruction, and, aside from God's merciful interference, hopelessly lost. Can such beings live together in society, with their discordant, repellant propensities and fierce desires, in unregulated, perpetual antagonism ? To unassisted human reason a benevolent solution of this question seems impossible. But God's wisdom in the great plan of redeeming fallen man has devised and ordained *government*, or the rule of the *superior* over the *inferior*, as one of his benevolent means for accomplishing that great end, and has given a code divinely regulated to prevent the abuse of power, while its use is made a means of the greatest good. He has placed man, wherever born, under some system of tutelage, from the cradle to the grave ; he has established a disciplinary scheme to train man, by physical restraint, to obedience and submission to law, and to the more elevated control of spiritual restraints, and thus, by a system of redemption devised in the councils of heaven, in which the end is man's salvation from the slavery of sin, man's terrestrial slavery is made one of the wisely-appointed means for giving him celestial and eternal liberty ; not the grovelling, earth-born, earth-bounded liberty claimed as an inalienable right, but the glorious spiritual liberty of the sons of God.

-

www.ingramcontent.com/pod-product-compliance
Lightning Source LLC
Chambersburg PA
CBHW031221290326
41931CB00036B/1329